ANTARCTICA AND THE ARCTIC
Facts, Figures, and Stories

BY JIM GIGLIOTTI

EXPLORING THE POLAR REGIONS TODAY

ANTARCTICA AND THE ARCTIC

Facts, Figures, and Stories

BY JIM GIGLIOTTI

MASON CREST

Mason Crest
450 Parkway Drive, Suite D
Broomall, PA 19008
www.masoncrest.com

Printed and bound in the United States of America.

First printing
1 3 5 7 9 8 6 4 2

Series ISBN: 978-1-4222-3863-9
ISBN: 978-1-4222-3865-3
ebook ISBN: 978-1-4222-7920-5

Library of Congress Cataloging-in-Publication Data on file with the publisher.

Developed and Produced by Shoreline Publishing Group.
Developmental Editor: James Buckley, Jr.
Design: Tom Carling, Carling Design Inc.
Production: Sandy Gordon
www.shorelinepublishing.com
Front cover: Adobe Stock Images/Nightman

QR Codes disclaimer:

CONTENTS

Key Icons to Look For

Words to Understand: These words with their easy-to-understand definitions will increase the reader's understanding of the text, while building vocabulary skills.

Sidebars: This boxed material within the main text allows readers to build knowledge, gain insights, explore possibilities, and broaden their perspectives by weaving together additional information to provide realistic and holistic perspectives.

Educational Videos: Readers can view videos by scanning our QR codes, providing them with additional educational content to supplement the text. Examples include news coverage, moments in history, speeches, iconic moments, and much more!

Text-Dependent Questions: These questions send the reader back to the text for more careful attention to the evidence presented here.

Research Projects: Readers are pointed toward areas of further inquiry connected to each chapter. Suggestions are provided for projects that encourage deeper research and analysis.

Series Glossary of Key Terms: This back-of-the-book glossary contains terminology used throughout this series. Words found here increase the reader's ability to read and comprehend higher-level books and articles in this field.

INTRODUCTION

Bundled in his down jacket, plastic boots on his feet, skis at the ready, explorer and adventurer Johan Ernst Nilson was struggling with his equipment at the North Pole when he had a sickening feeling: He could sense the ice was cracking beneath him. Seconds later, Johan was no longer standing on anything solid. He was in the frigid waters of the Arctic. He was tired, he was wet, he was freezing…and he still had 12 months of this journey to go!

Johan was just starting out on his yearlong trek from the North Pole to the South Pole—from the Arctic to the Antarctic. Those polar regions long have captured the imagination of real-life explorers and armchair adventurers alike. From the ancient Greeks in search of new lands in which to trade… to 19th-century explorers racing to become the first to reach the North and South Poles…to modern scientists and researchers studying the effects of climate change on our planet, the Arctic and the Antarctic have drawn men and women in search of adventure and knowledge.

But no one had ever gone all the way from one pole to the other until Johan did it on a trip that began in April of 2011 and ended in March of 2012.

Johan began by skiing 47 days from the North

When ice cracks underfoot of visitors to the Arctic regions, they might find themselves in freezing water.

Johan Ernst Nilson followed in the footsteps of a century-plus of adventurers who braved the elements of the North and South Poles.

Pole in the Arctic. He rode a bike through Canada and the United States. He also used kite-ski, sled, and sailboat as he navigated into South America, crossed the equator, and reached the South Pole in Antarctica. It wasn't all smooth sailing…or sledding. Johan fought through tropical hurricanes. He cracked his ribs. He suffered frostbite. And, of course, he fell into the icy waters of the Arctic. Although there was nothing funny about falling into the ice at the time, he can laugh about it now. "When it's minus-twenty de-

grees outside, it takes two days just to warm up!"

Yes, it does get to −20°F in the Arctic—and colder. Read on to learn just how much colder…and to learn other facts and figures about the Arctic and the Antarctic, as well as the stories of Johan and other adventurers past and present who explore the polar regions. We hope this book gives you an overview of the Arctic and the Antarctic that will inspire you to read more in the exciting series *Exploring the Polar Regions Today*.

Both polar regions are covered for many thousands of square miles by forbidding, ice-covered stretches.

Brrrr!

1

Words to Understand

balmy   mild

constellation   an arrangement of stars

fluctuates   shifts back and forth

hemisphere   the northern or southern half of the Earth as divided by the equator

morphs   changes in form

tongue-in-cheek   jokingly, sarcastically

Think it's cold where you live? Well, let's say you're in Buffalo, New York. It can get pretty chilly there. Winter temperatures in January average a high of about 31°F (–0.6°C). It's even colder in Minneapolis, where the high temperature averages 24°F (–4.4°C) in the first full month of winter. Of course, it's all relative: In Los Angeles, California, they consider it cold anytime the high thermometer reading dips below 60°F (15°C)—which it doesn't do very often. But all of that is nothing compared to the frigid conditions in the Arctic and the Antarctic.

The Poles

On a globe, the Arctic is at the very top, in the northern **hemisphere**. The Antarctic is at the bottom, in the southern hemisphere. The North Pole, then, is in the Arctic; the South Pole is in Antarctica. But while the South Pole is a fixed point of land (or, more precisely, ice-covered land), the North Pole is located in the middle of the Arctic Ocean. The water there is 13,400 feet (4,084 meters) deep. The ice sheets in the Arctic Ocean are up to 10 feet (3 meters) thick and always on the move, so there's no actual pole there! A pole planted in the ice could soon be miles away.

The Arctic is part of an area called the Arctic Circle. Scientists sometimes use the northern limit of the tree line as the border for the Arctic. The Arctic tree line is the northernmost point where trees can grow; beyond that, where it's too cold for trees, is tundra, a treeless area of plain with permanently frozen subsoil.

Antarctica is its own continent. Scientists believe that several hundred million years ago, the landmass on the Earth existed in one supercontinent called Pangaea. About 175 million years ago, the land began breaking into seven smaller continents. In addition to Antarctica, the other continents are Africa, Asia, Australia, Europe, North America, and South America.

The Arctic is water (the Arctic Ocean) surrounded by the land of North America, Russia, and Europe; the Antarctic is land (mostly covered in ice that can be up to three miles thick) surrounded by water.

This overhead view of a portion of the Arctic coastline shows well the flat plains of sea ice that ring the heavier concentrations of glaciers and ice masses.

The Arctic got its name from a Greek word (spelled "arktos" in English) meaning "bear." That's a reference to the **constellation** Ursa Major. Its most famous grouping of stars is commonly known as the "Big Dipper," but "ursa" was a Roman word meaning "bear," and the Greeks took their lead from that. Antarctica comes from the Greek "antarktos," which is a combination of "ante" and "arktos." In Greek, "ante" means "opposite." Antarctica is the polar opposite of the Arctic on the globe.

How Cold Is It?

The coldest temperature ever recorded on earth was –128.6°F (–89.2°C) in Vostok, Antarctica, on July 21, 1983. (By contrast, the average high temperature for Phoenix, Arizona, on that day each year is 106°F/41°C.)

Russian scientists brave one of the coldest places on Earth to maintain a science station at Vostok on the Antarctic continent.

The average temperature in Antarctica warms up to –58°F (–5°C) during the summer months—still not exactly **balmy** weather. The record low temperature for the Arctic is –90°F (–68°C), on a couple of different occasions in parts of Russia. The coldest temperature ever recorded in the United States came at Prospect Creek, Alaska, just above the Arctic Circle, in 1971: –80°F (–62°C).

The ordinary freezing point of water, of course, is 32 degrees Fahrenheit—*above* zero. (Thirty-two degrees Fahrenheit is zero degrees Celsius.) So there's no shortage of ice in the Arctic and the Antarctic!

Ice, Ice Baby

There's plenty of ice in the Arctic and Antarctica, but not all ice is created equal. There's frazil ice, grease ice, pack ice (also called sea ice), annual ice, multiyear ice, glaciers, icebergs, and lots, lots more. Who knew there were so many types of ice?

When the surface areas of seawater, like that in the Arctic Ocean, begin to freeze, they form a loose, slushy mixture called frazil ice. It **morphs** into grease ice, which is still thin and soupy, but sturdier than frazil ice. When grease ice thickens to a more solid version, it is pack ice. Pack ice that melts in the summer and then re-forms in winter is called annual ice. Pack ice that doesn't completely melt in the summer is called multi-year ice.

There are dozens of other types of ice, most of which are reflected in their name. Anchor ice is attached to the bottom of a sea or river. Brash ice consists of fragments from the wreckage of other ice. Tongue ice is the part of the ice edge that sticks out, sometimes as much as several kilometers. You can probably guess the shape of pancake ice.

When the fresh water of snow compacts into ice, like that in Antarctica, it forms massive, slow-moving shelves of ice called glaciers. Continental glaciers cover almost all of Antarctica: about 98 percent of it. But yes, there are still that 2 percent of ice-free areas in Antarctica. The largest ice-free region is called the McMurdo Dry Valleys.

An iceberg is a large chunk of floating ice that has broken off from a glacier. But there's a reason for the old saying that something is "just the tip of the iceberg"—meaning there is a lot more to an issue than you can see. About 90 percent of the size of an iceberg is below the surface of the water. The most infamous iceberg in history was the one that the British passenger ship

Just the Facts

	Arctic (incl. North Pole)	Antarctic (incl. South Pole)
Location	Latitude 90° North	Latitude 90° South
Avg. temp. (summer)	32°F (0°C)	−18°F (−28°C)
Avg. temp. (winter)	−40°F (−40°C)	−76°F (−60°C)
Area	5.4 million sq. mi. (14 million sq km)	6 million sq. mi. (15.5 sq km)
Coastline	25,000 miles (40,233 km)	18,000 miles (28,968 km)
Population	4,000,000	1,000–4,000

This photo shows, in a small way, the huge amount of solid ice in an iceberg that is submerged and thus invisible to passing ships.

Titanic struck in the North Atlantic Ocean in 1912. That iceberg had broken off from an Arctic glacier. The *Titanic*, which was making its first voyage and was thought to be unsinkable, went under less than three hours after hitting the iceberg. The disaster killed more than 1,500 passengers and crew members.

Polar Populations

How many people live in Antarctica? The short answer: none. Conditions are such that the full-time population at the South Pole is zero. In reality, the population of Antarctica **fluctuates** to include anywhere from about 1,000 to 4,000 people. That's the number of scientists, researchers, and visitors at the South Pole at any given time. It's at the high end of that number in the summer time, and the low end in the winter.

A British scientist brought to the Antarctic by the icebreaker in the background prepares ice core samples taken from deep beneath the ice surface.

The Sami people live in northern Russia and parts of Norway and Finland. This photo from the early 1900s shows their traditional clothing and dwelling.

Before European explorers reached the Arctic, a lot of people thought no one could live there, either, because of the harsh conditions. But as many as 5,000 years ago, the first Arctic settlers arrived, perhaps by crossing from Eurasia (the combined land mass of Europe and Asia) during an Ice Age. Those native tribes of the Arctic collectively are known as Inuit.

Inuit life in the Arctic

Time Travels

Time zones around the world are determined by the 24 imaginary lines of longitude that run from the North Pole to the South Pole. Since they all converge at one point, at the South Pole, you can stand in every time zone at once! You can't do that at the North Pole because, as noted, the exact point of the North Pole is under drifting sea ice.

So what time is it really at the South Pole? Well, because every time zone is represented, research stations often follow the time zone of their home country or that of the closest inhabited country. Many visitors simply use the time from whatever location they've traveled.

Today, about 4 million people live in the Arctic. They live in several different countries: the United States (parts of Alaska are in the Arctic Circle), Canada, Finland, Denmark (Greenland), Iceland, Norway, Russia, and Sweden. So while different countries own parts of the land, no one country can claim ownership of the Arctic.

In Antarctica, where there is no full-time population, no country owns the land. In the late 1950s, the 12 countries that were working in Antarctica (the United States, Argentina, Australia, Belgium, Chile, France, Japan, New Zealand, Norway, South Africa, the Soviet Union, and the United Kingdom) agreed to ban all military activity on the continent and to use the land cooperatively for scientific research. The Antarctic Treaty officially went into effect in 1961; by 2017, 53 countries were part of the agreement.

Similar...but Different

With so much ice, the Arctic and the Antarctic might appear to be similar—but they also have their own characteristics and distinctions.

Antarctica, for instance, is unique in that it is officially the world's largest desert. That doesn't seem right, but a desert is determined by amount of precipitation. Antarctica averages less than two inches (5.1 cm) of rain or snow each year. Annual precipitation in the McMurdo Dry Valleys: zero. In fact, the Dry Valleys have not had rain in two million years—winds that reach 200 miles per hour (320 km/h) suck away the moisture—making it officially the driest place on Earth.

The Arctic is called the "Land of the Midnight Sun." There is no sunshine in a winter that stretches for six months. On the other hand, there is no sunset in a summer that goes for the next six

Wet? Not really. Though covered with ice and snow, Antarctica gets very little annual precipitation, making it a sort of "ice desert."

Polar bears are probably the most well-know animal inhabitants of the Arctic Circle. They live around the world in the area above that geographic line.

months. The Alaska Goldpanners of the Alaska Summer League (a collegiate summer baseball league) even play an annual game in daylight…at midnight! The Midnight Sun Game during the June summer solstice needs no lights even though the game begins at 10 o'clock in the evening and goes until the early hours of the next morning. (Technically, the Fairbanks-based Goldpanners play south of the Arctic Circle.)

The Arctic is home to a variety of animal life, most notably huge polar bears, which can weigh upwards of 1,500 pounds (680 kg). (Fun fact: Polar bears can swim up to six miles (9.6 km) per hour…which would leave Olympic legend Michael Phelps in the dust!) Penguins, who live only in the southern hemisphere, are the most famous inhabitants of Antarctica. But the only land animals there generally can be seen only with the aid of a microscope. (Penguins often waddle around on the ice and land, but they are considered aquatic, flightless birds.) The occasional exceptions are the "elephants of Antarctica": a **tongue-in-cheek** reference to collembola, or springtails. They look like tiny insects. But at less than one millimeter in length—there are about 25 millimeters in an inch—these "elephants" are still pretty tough to spot.

 # Text-Dependent Questions:

1. What are the seven continents, and what was the name of the "supercontinent" from which they came?

2. What area of Antarctica is the driest place on Earth?

3. Name at least five of the eight countries in the Arctic Circle.

 # Research Project

Research the average monthly temperature in Antarctica, and plot your findings in one color on a graph. Then research the average monthly temperature in your hometown, and plot those findings in a different color on the same graph.

BRITISH ANTARCTIC TERRITORY

THADDEUS VON BELLINGSHAUSEN

Vostok

1p

This British postage stamp honors the Russian explorer Thaddeus von Bellinghausen, an early Antarctic explorer…probably!

Getting There

2

Words to Understand

cartographers   mapmakers

fabrications   things that are made up

paraphrased   when a person's words are not repeated exactly, but keep the same meaning

reputedly   according to reputation; supposedly

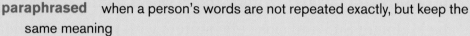

n 1820, when he sailed to within 20 miles (32 km) of the continent, Russia's Thaddeus von Bellingshausen was the first explorer to see Antarctica. Or was he? That same year, the British Royal Navy's Edward Bransfield and America's Nathaniel Palmer also claimed to be the first to see Antarctica. (Historians eventually sided with von Bellingshausen.) That set the tone for other polar debates to follow. In 1909, Robert Peary was the first man to reach the North Pole. Or was he? Frederick Cook claimed that he had already done it in 1908. (Historians eventually sided with Peary…mostly.) But only one person can ever be the first at something. What every explorer mostly seeks is the thrill of getting there.

In Quest of the North Pole

In 325 BCE, a Greek trader named Pytheas was likely the first European to reach the Arctic. None of his writings remain, so how do we know? Because some of his writings were quoted and **paraphrased** by later writers. In his works, Pytheas described the Midnight Sun and close encounters with polar ice. Pytheas' critics dismissed his observations as **fabrications** or as the stuff of fairy tales, but much of what he described turned out to be true.

By the time the Middle Ages were drawing to a close, Europeans were desperate to find a "Northwest Passage" for transporting the spices, silks, and other goods they obtained from the Far East. They hoped a Northwest Passage would prove to be a faster and easier way to get back and forth from Europe to India and Asia than the more difficult and slower trip around the southern tip of Africa.

Until 1869, when the Suez Canal linked the Red Sea to the Mediterranean Sea and made it possible for ships to sail from India to Western Europe, the only other way included dangerous, costly, and time-consuming land travel.

In 1497, John Cabot was the first of a series of explorers—eventually including Cabot's own son Sebastian in 1508—to search for the Northwest Passage. Another was Henry Hudson, after whom the Hudson River in New York is named.

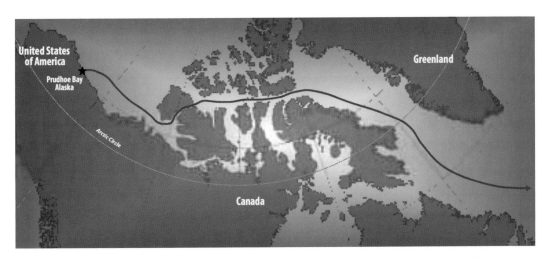

The red line shows the Northwest Passage from east to west. Europeans sought the west-to-east version for centuries.

A Northwest Passage wasn't discovered until the mid-1800s, and, after the Suez Canal was built, traversing it wasn't quite as urgent from a trading perspective. But the quest to achieve the feat didn't let up, and in 1903 Norwegian explorer Roald Amundsen set out in a relatively small fishing vessel outfitted with a gasoline engine. By the time Amundsen returned to his native country three-and-a-half years later, he had done it: He was the first to sail through a Northwest Passage.

On the way and back, Amundsen stopped for the winter in Nunavut in the Northwest Territories of Canada. The Inuit there taught him ways to survive the freezing cold, which would come in handy in later expeditions.

Amundsen had sailed through a Northwest Passage, but no one had yet reached the North Pole. In the late 19th century, Americans Frederick Cook and Robert Peary battled to become the first. For a time Cook and Peary were friends and shipmates: Cook had been a surgeon on Peary's Arctic expedition of 1891–92. Now they became rivals. In 1909, Peary returned from his final expedition claiming he had reached the North Pole—only to find that while he was away, Cook claimed to reach it one year earlier.

Historians have generally discredited Cook's claims of reaching the pole. While Peary's claims are more widely accepted, doubters say he may only have come close to the North Pole.

South Pole Explorers

The 1959 book called *The 100 Greatest Advertisements 1852–1958* includes a posting that Ernest Henry Shackleton **reputedly** ran in a London newspaper in 1900. "Men wanted for hazardous journey," the ad declared. "Low wages, bitter cold, long hours of complete darkness. Safe return doubtful. Honour and recognition in event of success."

Talk about truth in advertising! The explorers of Shackleton's time sure picked a dangerous way to seek fame and fortune. Sometimes these explorers failed on their expeditions and lived to tell about it. Sometimes they failed and never were heard from again. And sometimes search parties went after them, and never were heard from, either.

Despite the brutal honesty and dim outlook, Shackleton's ad supposedly brought an overwhelming response. Some 5,000 applicants responded, he once said, and he whittled down that number to a couple dozen or so possibilities. The real truth,

Almost as remarkable as the safe return of Shackleton's crew was the survival of many amazing images taken with glass plates, such as this one of his icebound ship.

though, is that Shackleton's ad probably is a myth, started by one of his early biographers. There is no surviving evidence that the ad ever actually ran.

What's not a myth is that Shackleton remains one of the most famous of the polar explorers. His exploits in saving a crew of 28 after his ship *Endurance* was wracked by the Antarctic ice in 1914 are legendary.

This set of statues in Oslo, Norway, honors Roald Amundsen (left) and some of the members of his crew who first made the trip to the South Pole.

Earlier, on his expedition aboard the *Nimrod* from 1907 to 1909, Shackleton came closer to the South Pole than anyone ever before. But he did not end up being the first to reach the South Pole. That honor belongs to Roald Amundsen. Remember those winter stops he made in Nunavut to and from the Northwest Passage? One of the things the Inuit taught him was to wear animal skins to combat moisture and cold instead of a traditional parka. He also learned to use sled dogs to get around.

That was important because in 1911, Amundsen was in a race with British naval officer Robert Falcon Scott to reach the South Pole first. Amundsen expertly guided his sled dogs while Scott was slowed by the ponies he also took with him.

Amundsen reached the South Pole in December 1911, planted Norway's flag in the ice, and returned home safely. Barely a month later, Scott was ecstatic finally to reach the South Pole—and was deflated to spot the flag and find that Amundsen had beaten him to it.

The story gets worse for Scott and his men: stuck in a blizzard on the way back to their base camp, they ran out of food and supplies and died.

Today's Travelers

It's not nearly so treacherous, of course, for modern travelers to reach the polar regions as it was for the explorers of the 19th and early 20th centuries. Many companies and tour operators offer trip packages that handle all the details. Still,

The Next Best Thing to Being There

The wooden cabin in which Sir Ernest Shackleton and his crew took refuge after leaving the *Nimrod* on their 1908 exploration can be seen on Google Street View.

Because of the extreme cold temperatures, the equipment and supplies in Shackleton's hut have remained remarkably well preserved. Books, clothing, canned foods, survival gear, and more—some 5,000 of the Shackleton team's personal possessions—are all visible in the Google panorama.

The company used a lightweight tripod camera with a fisheye lens to take various pictures of Shackleton's hut, which then were pieced together into a 360-degree image.

There are plenty of other Antarctic images available in Google Street View, too. In addition to looking at Shackleton's hut from 1908, you can also view Robert Falcon Scott's hut from 1911, see the flags from different nations planted in the ice at the Ceremonial South Pole, and check out the Cape Royds Adélie Penguin Rookery.

it's an expensive trip—and only for those physically capable of withstanding the harsh conditions.

But let's say you're a researcher and you've been asked by the National Science Foundation (NSF) to do some work at the South Pole. The NSF is the US government agency that supports research and education in science and engineering.

In Antarctica, that might mean helping hydrologists, who study the movement and quality of water that flows from glaciers after the round-the-clock sunshine of the continent's summer. Biological scientists study the microscopic organisms that survive in the harsh conditions of the Antarctic—maybe that means they survived the last ice age. Meteorologists study changes in the atmosphere and their effects. Other scientists study whales, penguins, the movement of glaciers, and lots, lots, more. Modern **cartographers** help other researchers safely navigate the continent.

In all, as many as 3,700 scientists work in as many as 40 research stations in Antarctica.

Whatever your specialty, though, you'll first need to get to Christchurch, the largest city on New Zealand's South Island. From Christchurch, it's an eight-hour flight to McMurdo Station, the largest of three US research stations in Antarctica—and, at up to 1,258 residents, the largest community on the continent. Anyone going to or from the South Pole passes through McMurdo.

Before you leave for McMurdo, though, you need to get outfitted at the Clothing Distribution Center in Christchurch. You can't even board the flight without goggles, a knit hat, a special red parka all scientists and visitors wear, wind pants, and "bunny boots" (insulated footwear).

After the eight-hour flight to McMurdo Station, on the southern coast of Antarctica, it's another several-hour flight to the Amundsen-Scott South Pole Station in the middle of the

The buildings of McMurdo Station spread out in a valley beneath rising Antarctic hills. The circular tanks contain fuel for the station and its vehicles.

Visitors in the official bright-orange clothing issue to Antarctic scientists deplane at McMurdo Station, ready for a long, chilly summer of work.

continent. The research station is named after the two explorers who reached the South Pole one month apart late in 1911 and early in 1912.

It's bright, cold, and windy at the South Pole. When the sun bounces off ice that stretches as far as the eye can see, many visitors are surprised by just how bright it is. So don't forget the sunglasses…and the long underwear!.

Text-Dependent Questions

1. Name the ancient Greek trader who likely sailed to the Arctic.

2. Who was the first man to reach the South Pole?

3. What US research station is the largest community on Antarctica?

 # Research Project

Write down as many different types of scientists you can think of who might work in Antarctica. Now imagine you are a scientist who has been asked to work at the South Pole. What would you like to study there?

Getting to McMurdo

Just how Santa Claus came to be connected with the North Pole is the subject of some mystery, but the jolly old elf has certainly helped put his "home" on the map.

The Polar Regions in Pop Culture

3

The lure of the polar regions long has attracted artists, musicians, photographers, and poets. It's no surprise, then, that Arctic and Antarctic life are as much a part of **pop culture** as that ice-cream bar you eat (you know, the Klondike bar with a polar bear on the wrapper) or that superhero movie you watch (the Batman series featuring the dastardly villain, The Penguin).

Polar Souvenirs

Nineteenth- and 20th-century polar expeditions set off a wave of interest in all things polar. Men such as Sir Ernest Shackleton, Sir John Franklin, and Richard Byrd became household names whose exploits were closely followed by newspaper readers around the world.

Not everyone could be an explorer, of course. So what was the next best thing to going to the Arctic? Bringing the Arctic to you!

Punch bowls, china plates, and ice cream dishes featured polar bears or other polar themes. Families played board games

Native handicrafts became popular souvenirs for visitors to the Arctic regions, such as this antique polar bear carved from whalebone.

This board game let young players—playing as the photographer McKinley—help the famous Admiral Richard Byrd during one of his many Arctic adventures.

in which their favorite explorer tried to reach the South Pole. Watch out for that iceberg! Avoid those blizzards! Don't get stranded without provisions!

In the early 1900s, tobacco companies produced trading cards of the top adventurers of the day, much as they did for star baseball players. On the front: a drawing of the explorer, or trinkets and souvenirs from his expedition. On the back: details of his greatest exploits.

William Bradford was a Massachusetts-born painter in the 19th century who was known for his Arctic landscapes. Paintings

American artist William Bradford painted what he saw on numerous voyages to the waters around the Arctic.

such as "The Icebergs" or "An Arctic Scene" weren't just created from his imagination, though. Bradford went on several Arctic expeditions himself. On one trip, his ship became locked in ice that spread hundreds of miles in all directions. For two weeks, he and his shipmates were stranded. But Bradford wasn't about to let the time go to waste. He sketched his surroundings, later published an account of the trip, and became one of the best-known artists of his time.

Rock On! . . . Quietly

In December 2013, scientists on Antarctica did the usual: studied
ice floes, observed plant and animal life, detected weather pat-
terns—and the unusual, attended a heavy-metal concert. That's

*The members of Metallica posed with the airplane that brought them south—way, way
south—for a memorable concert at an Antarctic research station.*

right, inside a small, clear, protective dome on an ice-free patch of land near the Carlini Scientific Base, the eight-time Grammy Award-winning group Metallica gave an hour-long concert it called, appropriately enough, "Freeze 'em All."

To shield concertgoers from the elements, organizers built an igloo-shaped protective enclosure that let in sunlight but kept out the freezing weather and high winds. The spectators packed into the venue. But instead of the tens of thousands of people that Metallica usually plays for, this crowd numbered about 120: scientists from various nations, plus winners of a contest sponsored by Coca-Cola. The crowd may have been small, but as the band noted on its Facebook page, "The energy in the little dome was amazing! Words can not describe how happy everyone was."

The concert presented lots of **logistical** challenges—a good reason why no such band ever had played in Antarctica before! One uncommon requirement: Metallica's usual amplification system couldn't be used. The ear-splitting, head-pounding music would have been damaging to the sensitive environment, and it would have violated international laws. So instead, attendees were given headphones over which the sound was transmitted.

While Metallica was the first world-renowned music act to play in Antarctica—and the first to play on all seven continents— live music is occasionally heard there. For instance, McMurdo Station, the largest United States research center on Antarctica, hosts periodic open-mic events at which scientists can showcase their musical skills.

More than 50 years before explorers walked on the Arctic, French author Jules Verne imagined their journeys; this drawing is from an edition of his book.

Ahead of His Time

Long before any European explorer ever set foot at the North Pole, Jules Verne imagined life in the Arctic with an adventure story called *A Winter Amid the Ice*. The famous French-born science fiction writer penned the story in 1854.

In *A Winter Amid the Ice*, an old sea captain sets out for the Arctic in search of his son, who was lost while trying to save another ship. The captain and his crew eventually lose their own ship to massive ice floes and have to go by foot and sled over the Arctic landscape. On his heroes' quest, Verne vividly describes floating mountains of ice, below-zero temperatures, overturning ice masses, and great white bears.

More than a decade later, Verne wrote a novel called *The Adventures of Captain Hatteras* (1866). It detailed the title character's obsession with reaching the North Pole, and the dangers that he and his crew encounter along the way.

Verne also wrote such widely read adventure novels as *Journey to the Center of the Earth* (1864), *Twenty Thousand Leagues Under the Sea* (1870), and *Around the World in Eighty Days* (1873). Sometimes called the "Father of Science Fiction," he had an imagination that was way ahead of its time.

Ho, Ho, Ho

Everyone knows that Santa Claus lives at the Arctic North Pole, right? Well, maybe not. Since the North Pole is not a fixed point on land, maybe he really lives in the town of North Pole, Alaska, or at Santa Claus Village in Rovaniemi, Finland, or even in Santa Claus, Indiana. The real Santa Claus, St. Nicholas of Myra, was a bishop in the fourth century in what is now the southern coast of Turkey.

Even if we're not exactly sure where Santa Claus lives, at least we know what he looks like. One of the first artists to characterize Santa Claus as a large, jolly fellow with a long gray beard was political cartoonist Thomas Nast in the magazine *Harper's*

Weekly in 1863. (That drawing, by the way, showed St. Nick as hailing from "Santa Clausville, N.P.")

Nast, who was born in Germany in 1840 but moved to New York City when he was six years old, also inked the elephant that has come to represent the Republican political party in the

The American artist Thomas Nash firmly fixed the visual identity of Santa Claus—red suit, white beard, and all—with a series of drawings in 1863.

United States. He often is credited with creating Uncle Sam, the **personification** of the US government, too. He did not create that, but he did popularize the image with his drawings.

Spy vs. Spy

Good guys…bad guys…a race against the Soviets to retrieve sensitive information. The 1968 motion picture *Ice Station Zebra* has all the elements of a typical Cold War-era spy film. But here's a twist: It all takes place on the ice and in the freezing waters of the Arctic. (The Cold War has nothing to do with the temperatures at

Rock Hudson (far right) and Ernest Borgnine (at bottom in brown) led a cast that played American soldiers defending the Arctic in Ice Station Zebra.

the poles. Instead, it was a period of more than four decades following World War II in which the United States and the Soviet Union did not trust each other and built up stockpiles of nuclear arms. The countries were never officially at war, but always **vigilant** about being prepared.)

In the movie, star Rock Hudson plays the captain of the *Tigerfish*. It's a US nuclear attack submarine that races the Soviets to retrieve a capsule containing secret film that both sides want to get their hands on. *Ice Station Zebra* was nominated for Academy Awards (the top motion-picture honors) for special effects and for the color cinematography that showed off the spectacular polar landscapes.

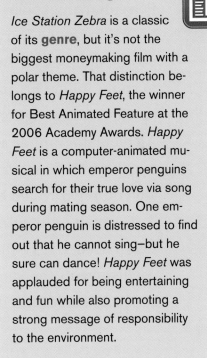

Dance King

Ice Station Zebra is a classic of its **genre**, but it's not the biggest moneymaking film with a polar theme. That distinction belongs to *Happy Feet*, the winner for Best Animated Feature at the 2006 Academy Awards. *Happy Feet* is a computer-animated musical in which emperor penguins search for their true love via song during mating season. One emperor penguin is distressed to find out that he cannot sing—but he sure can dance! *Happy Feet* was applauded for being entertaining and fun while also promoting a strong message of responsibility to the environment.

The movie was based on a novel of the same name by Alistair MacLean. The Scottish-born writer had first-hand knowledge of the Arctic. In the 1940s, during World War II, he served in Great Britain's Royal Navy. His missions included Arctic convoys that carried supplies to Russian troops there. (The Russians were on the Allies' side in World War II.)

Ice Station Zebra

#Pole2Pole

Pop culture met polar exploration when Johan Ernst Nilson made his trip from the North Pole to the South Pole in 2011–12. Johan posted updates on Twitter and his blog, so anyone who wanted to could follow his progress. He checked in with reporters via email, too. Highlights of his trek have been posted on YouTube. A cinematographer and a support car joined Johan on the trip, but the trek was mostly carbon footprint neutral because the adventurer traveled by ski, cycle, and sled.

German automobile manufacturer Audi sponsored the trip. Johan needed his equipment to be strong, light, and fast, so Audi used some of the same technology it puts in its cars to design specially made skis, bikes, and sleds.

Johan Ernst Nilson used a set of sleds that he pulled while he walked and skied across the Arctic to reach the North Pole in 2012.

Johan set out from the North Pole a little more than 101 years after Robert Peary reportedly stood there in 1909. He crossed through 17 countries on a trip that covered 20,000 miles, and he reached the South Pole on the 100th anniversary of Robert Falcon Scott's 1912 expedition. He drew inspiration from those adventurers, and others. "What all explorers have in common," he said, "is the will to reach a goal—the fight against what others think is impossible."

 # Text-Dependent Questions

1. What heavy-metal group was the first major music act to play a concert in Antarctica?

2. Name at least two of the famous adventure novels written by Jules Verne, the author of the short story *A Winter Amid the Ice*.

3. What penguin movie won the Academy Award?

 # Research Project

Look at a map of the globe and consider how you might travel from the North Pole to the South Pole (not by airplane!). How much of your route is via the ocean? How much is over land? How many miles per day would you need to travel to make it in one year, like Johan Ernst Nilson did?

US Secretary of State John Kerry examines that amazingly preserved artifacts in a cabin used by Antarctic explorer Ernest Shackleton.

In the News

4

Words to Understand

accessible   within reach

ice core   a sample removed from an ice sheet

inquisitive   curious

The Arctic and Antarctica have a long and storied history. But it's not all history books and grainy, black-and-white photos. Every day, it seems, there's something noteworthy going on at the poles. From US Secretary of State John Kerry's visit to Antarctica to an Arctic Report Card that highlights the effects of climate change, the polar regions are in the news.

Kerry's 2016 visit to the southernmost continent was intended to call attention to the ongoing climate change crisis, which is greatly affecting Antarctica.

State Trip

More than 100 years after Ernest Shackleton's early-20th-century journeys to Antarctica, US Secretary of State John Kerry stood in the hut that the famous explorer built to shield him and his crew from the elements.

Kerry was the highest-ranking American political official ever to visit Antarctica. His trip there in November 2016 also meant that he had visited both polar regions in his tenure as Secretary of State. One year earlier, he had spent time in Greenland in the Arctic.

In his role as Secretary of State from 2013 until early in 2017, Kerry's job was to carry out President Barack Obama's foreign policy. As part of that, he helped negotiate the Paris Agreement (drafted in 2015 and signed in 2016), in which more than 100 countries around the world teamed to combat climate change. Kerry visited Antarctica in 2016 to study the effects of climate change. Researchers there are studying the possibility that warmer ocean temperatures might weaken ice sheets and raise the sea level.

On his Antarctic trip, the Secretary of State hiked through frozen sections of the sea, got a bird's-eye view of the region on a helicopter tour, and peppered scientists with questions about their observations. There was time for a couple of touristy moments, too. In addition to checking out Shackleton's hut (and signing the guestbook there), Kerry whipped out his cell phone to video an **inquisitive** penguin that waddled up to his group to see what all the fuss was about.

Treasure Hunt

Imagine the awe of finding treasure that hasn't been touched by humans in more than 15 million years! That's exactly what

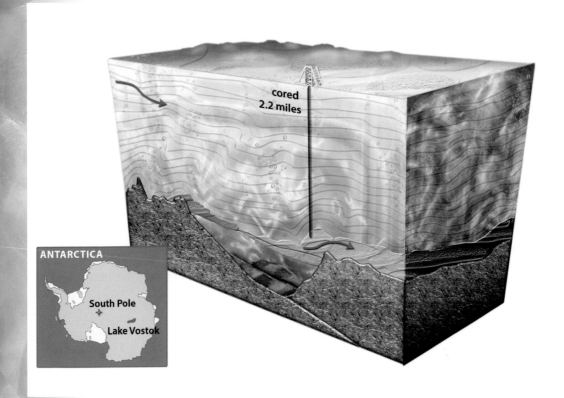

cored
2.2 miles

ANTARCTICA

South Pole

Lake Vostok

This diagram shows the miles-long drilling rig that dug into the ice at the bottom of Lake Vostok. Scientists will be studying history as they look at what they brought up.

happened to a team of Russian scientists in Antarctica in 2012. Their treasure: water.

After almost 20 years of trying, the Russian team reached the waters of Lake Vostok, more than 2 miles (3.2 km) beneath the surface of the Antarctic ice. Researchers estimate there are about 400 lakes under the Antarctic ice, and American teams (and others) are drilling to find them. But Lake Vostok is the oldest and largest of them all. It covers about 6,000 square miles

(15,540 sq km). That's 20 times the size of New York City! The **ice core** obtained from the drill was a record 12,400 feet (3,768 m) in length.

In such extreme conditions, scientists didn't expect to find much in the way of life. And the first water samples obtained from the lake were contaminated by compounds intended to keep the borehole from collapsing or freezing. But after analyzing the ice core from lake water that froze to the bottom of the glacial ice, scientists were surprised to find more than 3,500 living organisms. Some were single-cell and multi-cell organisms. Why is that important? Because scientists know that such organisms existed on Earth before plants and animals did. And if those organisms could adapt and survive in a subglacial ecosystem on our planet, they might very well survive in other systems we previously thought impossible—such as under the ice crust on planets or their moons far from our sun. Jupiter, anyone?

Arctic Report Card

In December 2016, the US Department of Commerce's National Oceanic and Atmospheric Administration (NOAA) released its annual Arctic Report Card. It represents the findings of 61 scientists from 11 nations around the world. The report found that warmer air temperatures above the Arctic were delaying annual sea ice freezing and "leading to extensive melting of Greenland ice sheet and land-based snow cover." Among other findings related to climate change:

- The average annual air temperature over land areas in the Arctic was the highest ever observed, and represented an increase double the rate of global temperature increase.

- Spring snow cover in the North American Arctic set a record low since satellite observations began in 1967.

- Arctic ice is thinning and sea surface temperatures are rising.

Source: NOAA.gov

Mystery Solved

Sometime in 2009, an Inuit man on a fishing trip in the Canadi-an Arctic spotted something poking up out of the ice. Strangely, it looked like the mast of ship. The man took some photos, but when the camera was later ruined, he figured it was the end of the story.

But in 2016, the man, a Canadian Ranger, mentioned his tale to the leader of a research vessel sailing in the waters of King William Island. The Arctic Research Foundation pursued the lead,

This painting imagines the scene as members of the John Franklin crew race to try to save one of their ships. Both vessels were lost to the ice, however.

Canadian scientists and divers discovered Franklin's HMS Terror, *remarkably preserved in the icy waters for more than a century.*

and found an almost perfectly preserved ship buried in about 80 feet of water. It was the HMS *Terror*, one of two ships on Sir John Franklin's ill-fated 1845 expedition in search of a Northwest Passage. All 129 men aboard the *Terror* and the *Erebus* (the latter had been found two years earlier, about 30 miles away from the site of *Terror*) died when the ships became stuck in ice in 1846 and they had to try to hike to safety.

At the time of the tragedy, several search expeditions failed to turn up any sign of the men, and the ships long had been considered lost forever.

Rescue!

On the last day of November in 2016, an 86-year-old man visiting the South Pole with his tour group became ill with altitude sickness and had to be airlifted to safety. A grueling eight hours later, he arrived at a hospital in New Zealand. The man was the famed astronaut Buzz Aldrin.

Tourists such as Aldrin have been visiting Antarctica since the late 1950s. Early visitors, though, hitched a ride on naval vessels

A ski-equipped cargo airplane like this one was used to rescue former astronaut Buzz Aldrin from Antarctica when he became sick during a tourist visit there.

resupplying the region; the first ship strictly for fare-paying passengers was in 1969. Today, more than 100 companies from around the world are part of the International Association of Antarctic Tour Operators (IAATO), which bring nearly 40,000 travelers a year to the region.

Aldrin, the man who walked on the moon after Neil Armstrong on the Apollo 11 space flight in 1969, was rescued from the Amundsen-Scott South Pole Station by the 109th Air Wing (109 AW) of the New York Air National Guard. The 109 AW flew him to McMurdo Station on the Antarctic coast on a ski plane—an aircraft equipped with ski gear instead of wheels for takeoff and landing in the Arctic and the Antarctic. The 109 AW is the only unit in the world that flies the aircraft.

The airplane wasn't called into action just because Aldrin is a famous astronaut. As the airlift support to the National Science Foundation scientific research mission, it's been making such daring rescues for a long time. Personnel at the science stations in Antarctica, for instance, can handle basic medical care and stabilize injuries, but "we do these [airlifts] as a matter of routine sometimes because [the science stations] don't have the capability to deal with some things," said Air National Guard Lt. Col. David Panzera after Aldrin was rescued.

It may be routine to the 109 AW, but not to most people. Winter evacuations are especially dangerous, but even summer rescues such as Aldrin's (remember, Antarctica is in the southern hemisphere, so winter and summer months are opposite those

With climate change opening new sea lanes and areas of open water, larger ships are making their way into the Arctic in search of oil.

in the United States) pose difficulty because of the elevation and wind—not to mention the still freezing temperatures.

In 1999, the 109 AW famously rescued a research scientist at the South Pole who was suffering from breast cancer. In 2001, a science station doctor came down with a life-threatening case of pancreatitis. There was an Australian researcher with a broken leg in 2008, critically injured Japanese sailors in 2012, and many others. "We've made, in essence, a dangerous mission safe," Panzera said.

Their stories, like Aldrin's, had a happy ending. After one week, he was released from the hospital and returned to the United States. And his name made the history books again: He was the oldest person ever to make it to the South Pole.

Black Gold

The rapidly melting ice in the Arctic, which is almost certainly an effect of climate change caused by humans, has made drilling for oil in the region more **accessible**. That's good news for oil companies, but not so much for environmentalists who foresee a host of problems that petroleum exploration might bring. Oil exploration in the Arctic is more technologically challenging than other areas not only because of the harsh climate, but especially because of environmental concerns. An oil spill could be disastrous.

But there's a lot of money to be made in oil exploration—some experts believe the Arctic contains 25 percent of the undiscovered oil in the world—and the United States, Russia, Canada, and Denmark (Greenland) all have made territorial claims to drilling in the Arctic. That's sure to spark major political squabbling. More than one newspaper has even called petroleum exploration in the Arctic the "new Cold War."

Oil in the Arctic

Though the US has banned oil exploration in its territorial waters, Russia has not done the same and continues to explore a wider and wider area for oil reserves.

In 2016, President Barack Obama permanently banned oil drilling from some parts of the territorial waters of Alaska that are inside the Arctic Circle. Environmentalists were overjoyed, but it remains to be seen how permanent the ban will actually be as oil companies continue to seek new drilling sites.

While the United States was—at least at that point—turning away from oil exploration, Russia was expanding its footprint. In 2015, it began construction of a large military base on Alexandra

Land Island, complete with troop living quarters and vehicle storage. Called the Arctic Trefoil after its three-winged shape, the base is the largest permanent structure in the Arctic. In 2017, Russian president Vladimir Putin visited to add new emphasis on his country's designs toward the region.

You can read more about Arctic petroleum exploration in Michael Centore's *Oil and Gas in the Arctic* in the Exploring the Polar Regions Today series.

 # Text-Dependent Questions

1. Who was the highest-ranking American government official ever to visit Antarctica?

2. Name one reason it is significant that scientists found living organisms in Lake Vostok beneath the Antarctic ice.

3. What British explorer's long-lost ship was found in September 2016 after 170 years in the Arctic waters?

 # Research Project

Research and write a short report about the potential problems and side effects of oil exploration in the Arctic. What kinds of alternative energy solutions might be available in the region?

FIND OUT MORE

Websites

www.timeforkids.com/minisite/antarctica
Learn about Antarctica and the research that's happening there.

polardiscovery.whoi.edu/index.html
The website of the Woods Hole Oceanographic Institution has lots of information about the Arctic and the Antarctic.

Books

Goodman, Susan E., with photographs by Michael J. Doolittle. *Life on the Ice*. Minneapolis, MN: Millbrook Press, 2006.

Hamilton, S.L. *Polar Exploration (Xtreme Adventures)*. Edina, MN: ABDO & Daughters, 2014.

Nichols, Catherine. *Polar Adventures (True Tales)*. New York: Children's Press, 2003.

Revkin, Andrew C. *The North Pole Was Here: Puzzles and Perils at the Top of the World*. Boston: Kingfisher, 2006.

SERIES GLOSSARY OF KEY TERMS

circumpolar: the area surrounding the North Pole, including the Arctic regions

Cold War: when nations are openly hostile toward each other while not resorting to physical warfare

continental shelf: the relatively shallow seabed surrounding a continent; the edge of a continent as it slopes down into the sea

indigenous: native or original to a particular place

floe: an ice sheet floating in the water

meterology: the study of weather

pelts: furred animal skins

permafrost: a layer of soil that stays frozen all year long

province: an area in Canada with its own name and government, similar to a state

subsistence: a basic, minimal way of living, with only things that are necessary to survive

sustainable: something that can be maintained or practiced for a long duration without negative effects

taiga: a biome that includes the forest of mostly evergreen trees found in the southern Arctic regions

territorial waters: the parts of an ocean over which a country has control

tundra: a type of biome in very cold areas characterized by limited plant growth, frozen soil, and low rainfall

INDEX

PHOTO CREDITS

ABOUT THE AUTHOR

Jim Gigliotti is a freelance author who lives in sunny southern California. A former editor at the National Football League, he has written more than 75 books for youngsters on nonfiction topics ranging from sports to presidents to medieval knights and more.